FIFTY FAVOURITE
BIBLE STORIES

IN THE CARPENTER'S SHOP

FIFTY FAVOURITE
BIBLE STORIES

EDITED BY
ERNEST H. HAYES

THE RELIGIOUS EDUCATION PRESS LIMITED
(*A member of the Pergamon Group*)

HEADINGTON HILL HALL   OXFORD

First printed 1947
Reprinted   1953
Reprinted   1957
Reprinted   1964
Reprinted   1970
Reprinted   1973

08 006196 6

PRINTED IN GREAT BRITAIN BY OFFSET LITHOGRAPHY
AND REPRINTED BY A. WHEATON & CO., EXETER, DEVON

CONTENTS

GOD MAKING THE WORLD

Genesis **1**. 1–3, 5, 10, 14–18.

HAVE you ever wondered about the long ago days, before you, or your mother and father, or any other people were born? Before there were any kittens or puppies, any birds or flowers or grass or trees? *'In the beginning there was always God.'*

When everywhere was filled with cloud and mist and fire, God was over all. He was loving and kind, and He planned to make the wonderful world.

When the time came, God's hand shaped the world from the cloud and the mist and the fire, and He set it spinning on its path. His hand guided it, and has guided it on its path ever since.

Yet the earth was still dark and bare. There was no life upon it and it was very empty. And God said, 'Let there be light: and there was light. And God saw the light, that it was good: and God divided the light from the darkness. And God called the light Day, and the darkness He called Night.'

By day God gave the sun to give light and warmth to the round earth. In the night sky He set the moon and the stars with their soft, restful light. Each had its own path and moved as God commanded.

Some day, when men and women and little children would live upon the earth, these lights would be friendly guides to light up the dark earth and show people the way to go. The sun would help the flowers to grow, and would bring colour to the cheeks of little children. The dim light of night would be a soft curtain shutting out the brightness, and helping tired people to sleep.

And God divided the land from the sea, and set bounds beyond which the sea must not go.

God knew that some day little children would like to play at the edge of the sea, and that the sun and the sea would make them strong and happy.

How glad we are that He made the sun, the moon and the stars; and that He gave us the blue sea with its waves and sandy beach!

THE GARDEN HOME

Genesis **2**. 8–10, 18, 19.

GREAT wide, beautiful, wonderful world,
  With the wonderful water round you curled,
  And the wonderful grass upon your breast—
World, you are beautifully drest.

The wonderful world was ready to be a home for God's children. The Heavenly Father had given it its beautiful dress. He had caused grass to grow for the cattle, and plants for the service of man.

The world was like a garden, but it waited for some-one to live in it.

All kinds of living creatures began to appear, and in time animals crept on the ground, insects fluttered among the flowers, and birds flew in the air. Furry animals found their homes in caves in the rocks, or among the branches of the trees. Fish swam in the sea and in the rivers.

Last of all came man, and there began to be homes on the round earth. Men and women worked for one another—men seeking food by hunting and fishing, women tending the garden and caring for the babies born to them.

God made men and women strong enough and wise enough to find out many secrets. How to take the wild animals and tame them and teach them to be their helpers and friends. How to learn the ways of plants, and to find out which were good for food. How to make fire, how to hollow a tree-trunk and make a boat, how to make a house of tree-trunks and branches, how to make clothing of skins.

These were all secrets that God helped men and women to find out.

God Who had made them, helped men and women to learn about Himself. He talked to them in the wind and the storm, in the sounds of the sea and the stream, and in the silence of the starry night. They began to think about God and to listen to Him.

They often made mistakes, like you do over your lessons. But God is the most patient of teachers.

'Like as a father pitieth his children, so the Lord pitieth them that fear Him.' The Heavenly Father loved His children, and He has gone on loving them ever since. He is still helping us to find out more of His secrets. Still talking to us if we will listen.

God Who made the grass,
The flower, the fruit, the tree,
The day and night to pass,
Careth for me.

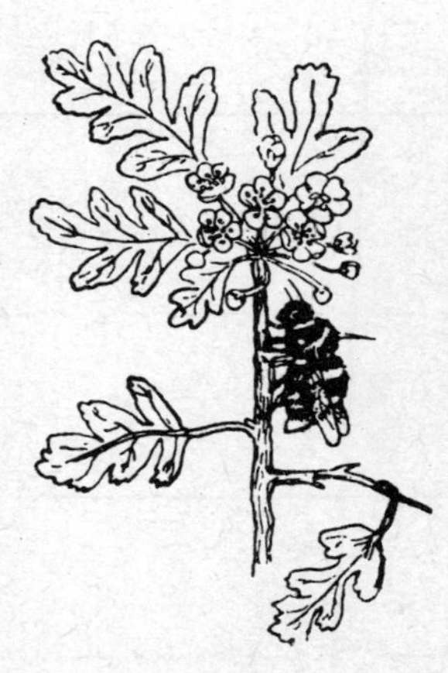

A STORY OF A TENT HOME

Genesis 13. 18; 18. 1–8; 21. 1–3.

HERE is a story about Abraham that the teacher often told Jesus and the other boys at the school at Nazareth.

Abraham had such large flocks of sheep and cattle that he had to move from place to place in order to supply them with food. When the sheep and cattle had eaten the grass in one little valley, they had to be led over the hills to the next valley where the grass was long and fresh.

So Abraham could not live in a stone or brick house. He had to have a home which could be easily carried about on the backs of camels. He lived in a large tent, made of skins of animals, sewn together, and stretched over poles, and held in position by strong ropes. This made a comfortable home which kept out wind and rain, and when Abraham had to move on to another place it was easy to take down and carry away.

One day Abraham made a new camp on a great grassy plain. It was a splendid place to make his home, for there was enough grass to last the herds for a long time, and plenty of fresh cool water for them to drink.

Abraham and his wife, Sarah, thought they would like their new tent-home very much, but there was one thing they wanted to make them *quite* happy. They had no children of their own, and they did so want a little son.

Abraham was sitting in the shadow of the tent door one very hot day, when he saw, to his surprise, three men coming towards the tent. He got up and ran towards them, bowing himself to the ground.

'Do not go away,' he said, 'but rest under this tree for a while. I will have water fetched to wash your feet, and will bring you food, so that you may refresh yourselves.'

The three strangers sat down under the shady tree while Abraham and Sarah hurriedly prepared a meal.

When it was ready Abraham served it himself to the strangers under the tree. While they were eating, one of them said to Abraham: 'Where is your wife, Sarah?'

'She is in the tent,' replied Abraham.

Then the stranger made a wonderful promise to Abraham: 'God is going to send you and your wife, Sarah, a baby son very soon,' he said.

Sarah was standing behind the tent door-curtain, and could hear all that was said, though she could not be seen. When she heard the stranger's promise she laughed aloud for joy.

So Abraham discovered that in being kind to strangers he had been welcoming the messengers of God to his tent-home; and he was very glad.

Sure enough, a few months later, God sent Abraham and Sarah a baby boy of their very own; just as the stranger had promised. They were so very happy, that they called the baby Isaac, which means 'Laughter.'

'God has made me laugh with joy,' said Sarah as she kissed her little son, 'so that all who hear may laugh with me.'

THE STORY OF A JOURNEY

Genesis 24.

ISAAC had grown into a tall young man, when one day his father, Abraham, called his most trusted servant to his tent. He made him sit down beside him, then said solemnly: 'I want you to go on a long journey, to the city of Ur, from which I came, and find a wife for Isaac, my son, from among my own people. I am too old to go such a long journey myself, so you must go for me.'

Eliezer was very proud to be sent on such an important errand for his master.

Early next morning he said good-bye to Abraham, and climbed on to the back of a camel. He had nine other camels laden with food and water for the journey, and beautiful gifts for the bride and her parents.

One evening, after many days' travel across the hot sandy desert, Eliezer saw the houses and temples of the city of Ur in the distance. Just outside the city was a well, surrounded by trees. Eliezer made his camel kneel down there, and he climbed from its back.

Kneeling down under one of the trees, Eliezer prayed to God to help him to choose the right wife for Isaac; then he sat down near the well to rest. Before long he saw a young girl coming out of the city to fetch water from the well. Eliezer was so tired and thirsty. 'I will ask her for a drink,' he thought.

When the girl had filled her water-jar, Eliezer said: 'I pray you let me drink a little water from your pitcher.'

'Why, yes, drink as much as you like,' replied the girl, and when he had finished drinking she said: 'Now I will draw water for your camels, too.' She emptied her pitcher into a trough and ran back to the well to refill it. Again and again she filled the trough until all the thirsty camels had finished drinking.

As Eliezer watched her, he thought: 'This girl would surely make a good wife for Isaac. She is kind to draw water for me and all my camels; and she is beautiful too.' Taking the gold bracelet and ear-rings from a leather bag, he gave them to the girl, and asked her name and whether he could stay at her mother's house.

'My name is Rebekah,' she replied, 'and my brother's name is Laban. We have plenty of room for you, and straw and food for the camels.'

So Eliezer went with Rebekah to her home, and her mother and brother brought him food and drink. But Eliezer would not eat until he had delivered his message, and given Rebekah the beautiful presents he had brought. Then he asked her if she would go back with him to be Isaac's wife.

Rebekah promised to go with Eliezer, and next morning they started on the long journey back to Canaan. It took many days, but at last they arrived one evening at the camp. Isaac welcomed Rebekah gladly, and she became his wife and he loved her very much.

Eliezer was very happy, too, and thanked God for helping him in his search, and for bringing him safely back to his master.

JACOB AND THE ANGELS

Genesis **28.** 10–22.

LONG, long ago a young man, named Jacob, set out on a great journey alone. He had to leave his mother and father and his home because he had wronged his brother Esau, and deceived his father. Esau was very angry and vowed to be revenged, so Jacob had to hurry away secretly, as fast as he could.

It was dangerous to travel alone, for wild animals might attack him, and robbers lay in wait for lonely travellers. So Jacob felt very much afraid as he hurried along the lonely mountain path. He was going far away to the north where his uncle Laban lived.

All that day Jacob hurried on, anxious to get as far away as possible from his home and his brother before nightfall. Even during the hot afternoon he dared not rest, but when the sun began to sink behind the mountains, Jacob knew that he must look round for a safe place in which to spend the night.

By this time he had reached a wide valley strewn with large stones. He found some dry sticks and leaves, and lit a fire to keep off wild animals. He drank some water from a little spring, and ate a cake of bread, then lay down to rest, using a large stone for a pillow.

Jacob was so tired that he soon fell fast asleep. Then he had a wonderful dream. He dreamt that he saw a ladder reaching from earth to heaven; on it angels were going up and down, and he saw God standing above. In his dream he heard God speaking to him:

'I am the God of your grandfather Abraham, and of your father Isaac; to you and to your children I give this land where you are lying. I will guard you wherever you go, and I will bring you back safely to this land! I will never leave you till I have done what I have promised.'

Then Jacob awoke; day was breaking and the valley was filled with grey shadows. 'Surely the Lord must be here,' he said, 'and I never knew it. This is none other than the House of God, and this is the gate of Heaven.'

Then he took the stone which he had used as a
pillow and set it up on end to be a stone of remem-
brance. He made a promise that he would always
worship God and obey His laws. Then he went on
his journey again, happy and comforted, knowing
that God was with him wherever he went.

BABY MOSES

Exodus 2. 1–10.

LONG, long ago, in a tiny little house by the great River Nile, there lived a mother and a father, a sister who was twelve, whose name was Miriam, and a little brother who was three, and whose name was Aaron.

Then a new baby came to live in that little home, a beautiful baby boy. They would all have been very happy about the baby but for one thing. In that land there was a cruel king. This king had said that none of the boy babies of the Hebrew people could be allowed to live.

Miriam's mother and father were Hebrews, and they all wondered very much how they could hide him. They managed till he was three months old. Then God told the mother a splendid plan.

She bade Miriam gather an armful of the tall rushes that grew by the river-side. Then she wove these into a big basket-cradle.

When the cradle was finished, the mother smeared it inside and out with pitch to keep out the wet. When it was dry she put a little blanket inside.

Then Miriam and her mother went down to the river-side—Miriam carried the baby and the mother the cradle-boat. Then they put the baby in the cradle-boat, and found a safe place among the rushes, where they put the baby in its strange new bed. Miriam stayed close by to watch.

Presently the princess came down to the river to bathe. She saw something in the water, and sent one of her ladies-in-waiting to see what it was. The lady lifted the baby out of his cradle, and he began to cry. The princess spoke kindly to the baby, and clever Miriam then came out from her hiding-place behind the rushes and said: 'Shall I fetch a nurse to nurse the baby for you?' And Pharaoh's daughter said: 'Go.' Then Miriam ran and called her mother. When the baby's mother came, the princess said: 'Take this child and nurse it for me, and I will give thee thy wages.' And the woman took the child and nursed it. And the child grew, and she brought him to the princess and he became her son. And she called his name Moses, and said: 'Because I drew him out of the water.'

MOSES AND THE SHEPHERDESSES

Exodus **2**. 15–21.

WE often hear about shepherds in the Bible. This story is about seven maidens who tended their father's sheep—shepherdesses.

They lived in a lonely and quiet land called Midian. They had tents for houses, and every day they took their father's flock to seek pasture.

At midday they led their flocks to the well. Now the well was covered with a large, flat, round stone, and the custom was to wait till all the shepherds had gathered, and then one would lift off the stone.

One day they came to the well, drew water in their pitchers after the stone was lifted, and filled the troughs to water the flocks.

But some rude shepherds came up, and drove them away, and began to get water for their own flocks.

A stranger was sitting near the well, and when he saw the rude, rough shepherds he came up and himself drew water for the seven shepherdesses to help them. The shepherds must have been ashamed, for they let the stranger go on with the work.

The troughs were filled and re-filled till all the sheep had had enough.

When the shepherdesses went back to their tent home, their father said: 'How is it that ye are come so soon to-day?' They said: 'An Egyptian saved us from the rough shepherds and he also drew water for us, enough for all the flock.'

The father said: 'Where is he? Why have you left the man? Call him that he may have supper with us.'

So the maidens fetched the stranger from Egypt, and he had supper in their father's tent. They learnt that his name was Moses. He was the very same you read about last time, who had been put in the ark among the rushes. His sister was Miriam, and the princess had made him her son.

But now he had come to the land of Midian. And he married one of the seven shepherdesses and became a shepherd himself. By and by he and his wife had a little son of their own who grew and played merrily among the tents and flocks.

FOOD AND WATER IN THE DESERT

Exodus 16. 1–4.

LONG, long ago a great host of people went a long journey through the wilderness. It was bare and stony. Very few trees grew there and it was very hard to find enough grass for the flocks and herds, for the people had sheep and goats and asses and oxen.

Worse still there was very little water. There were scarcely any streams and very few wells. No one could get a drink, as you can, just by turning a tap. The people who went on this journey were called the Children of Israel. Their leader was Moses. The same Moses we read about last time who helped the shepherdesses draw water for their flocks. The same Moses whose mother put him in a cradle-boat, or ark, among the rushes by the River Nile.

Now Moses was an old man, and he was God's servant. He was taking the Children of Israel to the Land of Canaan. Sometimes they were very, very hungry, and then they grumbled at poor Moses.

Moses prayed to God to help them, and God helped them. Next morning, when the fathers and mothers and boys and girls woke up, on the ground they saw something small and round like seeds, and a good deal like hoar frost. 'What is it?' the people asked one another.

Moses said: 'It is the bread which God has given you to eat.' So the people gathered it in baskets. Then they ground it in hand-mills, or beat it in a mortar, and baked it in pans and made cakes of it. And so the people had food to eat. They called this food *Manna*.

One day they had no water to drink. Their water-pots were empty and the country was dry and hot and hard. They went three days and found no water.

Then they came to a place called Marah where was a stream. Full of joy they tasted the waters—but found them bitter.

The people grumbled very loudly, saying to Moses,
'What shall we drink?' He prayed to God to help
him and God shewed him a bush, which, put in the
water, sweetened it.   So the people were able to drink,
and to fill their water-pots for the next part of their
journey.   And Moses and they thanked God for His
gifts of water and food.

THE TENT CHURCH

Exodus **35**. 4–29.

MOSES was the leader of the Children of Israel in their journey through the Wilderness to the Land of Canaan. He was their teacher as well. He taught them about God, and prayed to God for them.

Often all the people gathered at the foot of a mountain to listen to what Moses had to say. God gave Moses the words to say.

They had no Church to go to—just the big out-of-doors. But often they had the feeling that God was with them there. He was on the mountain-side, or at night He seemed to dwell among the stars that shone so brightly in the sky.

But they began to think that they would like to build a special house where He might dwell. They moved about from place to place, so it could not be a house of stone. It had to be a house of hair, a tent. People call it the *Tabernacle*, which just means the *Tent*.

Moses called the people together and talked to them about this Church which he and they wanted to make.

'Whoever is of a willing heart,' he said, 'let him bring an offering. He can bring gold, or silver, or brass; or curtains of blue, purple and scarlet; or fine linen, or goats' hair cloth, or choice wood, or olive oil for the light, or precious stones.'

All the people went away to see what they could find to give. Later they came, every one whose heart stirred him up, and they brought the Lord's offering. And they came, both men and women, and brought brooches, and earrings, and rings and other jewels. And some brought blue and purple and scarlet cloth for curtains, others brought fine linen, others gave goats' hair cloth to make the walls of the Tabernacle. Those who had specially beautiful wood brought it.

And all the women that were wise-hearted did spin

with their hands, and brought that which they had
spun.   Others dyed the cloth that was spun with blue
and purple and scarlet dyes.   The children helped to
fetch and carry and to take messages.   They watched
the grown-ups at work and asked many questions
about the Tent Church, the first Church they had
ever seen.   So Moses finished the work.   Then a
cloud covered the Tent of Meeting, and the glory of
the Lord filled the Tabernacle.

RUTH THE GLEANER

Ruth 2.

LONG, long ago, in the city of Bethlehem, there lived a lovely girl whose name was Ruth. Ruth had come to Bethlehem from a far-off land, to care for her mother Naomi, who was poor, and sad and lonely.

'I will work for you, Mother,' said Ruth to Naomi.

The harvest was golden in the fields when Ruth came to Bethlehem. So she said to her mother: 'Let me now go to the fields and glean there.'

Now the kind custom of those days was to allow poor folks to go to the fields and gather the barley or wheat from the corners, and keep that for themselves. The 'gleaners,' as they were called, were allowed to pick up the ears of corn that fell when the reapers were tying up the sheaves. And when the harvest had been cut by the scythes, the gleaners might go and gather any ears that were left.

Ruth wanted to be a gleaner, and Naomi said: 'Go, my daughter.' She went to the fields that belonged to rich farmer Boaz.

The farmer came and said to the reapers: 'The Lord be with you,' and they answered: 'The Lord bless thee.' Then said Boaz to his servant who was set over the reapers: 'Whose daughter is this?' The servant answered: 'This is Ruth who came from Moab to care for Naomi.'

Then the farmer turned to Ruth and said: 'Glean in my field so long as you can. If you are thirsty, drink from that which is set for my reapers.' And at meal-time Boaz said to Ruth: 'Come hither, and eat of the food set for my young men.' And when she went to glean he said: 'Let her glean among the standing sheaves, and pull out some for her on purpose.' So Ruth gleaned in the field until the evening, and she beat out the ears that she had gleaned, and there was a great measureful of grain.

Her mother was delighted, and told her that Boaz was a relation of theirs. Every day while the barley harvest lasted, Ruth gleaned in his field. And all through the wheat harvest, too.

By and by Boaz took Ruth to be his wife, and Naomi went to live at the cosy farm-house, too. And one day Naomi held the baby son of Ruth and Boaz in her arms.

THE BOY WHO HEARD GOD'S VOICE

1 Samuel 3. 1–10.

DO you remember how the Tent of Meeting came to be made, and how the children helped in making it? Our story now is about a boy who served in a house built for God, called the Temple.

A long while after the first Tent of Meeting was made, the people called Israelites came to their new homeland. They built houses for themselves, for they no longer wanted to travel about with tents from one place to another. And soon they built a house for God—a meeting-place of wood and stone, and they called it the Temple. On sabbath days the people came, and the Temple priest taught them to pray and worship.

One day a little boy came to the Temple. He was brought by his mother to the old priest, Eli.

'This is my boy, Samuel,' said the mother. 'I want him to learn to serve God in this Temple. Will you take him for your helper?'

Eli, the old priest, was glad to have Samuel's willing hands to help and quick feet to run on his errands. Samuel soon learned how to help the old priest. It was good to be able to help Eli, but Samuel loved helping in the Temple most of all. He liked the days when Eli led the worship there, and men and women came to pray to God.

It was quiet in the Temple and often as Samuel dusted the beautiful gold and silver vessels on the altar and swept the floor clean he thought of God, whose house it was. He loved cleaning and filling the seven-branched lamps with oil. They were shaped like big candle-sticks, and when each tiny lamp in them was lighted, they looked in the dark Temple like wonderful great flowers with lights for blossoms.

At night Samuel closed the doors of the Temple, and in the morning he opened them, letting in the sunshine and the cool morning air. There were so many things to do for God and for Eli, that Samuel was busy all day. At night he put down his mattress

on the floor and went straight off to sleep, while the
Temple lights on the altar shone in the darkness.
And all night Samuel would sleep, nor wake until
the morning.

One night Samuel closed the Temple doors as
usual, lit the little lamp, and then went to bed. He
had been asleep for some time when he was awakened
by a voice calling him.

'Here am I,' cried Samuel, as he jumped up and
ran to Eli's room.   'Here am I, for you called to me.'

'No,' said Eli, 'I did not call you. Go and lie
down again.'

Samuel went back to his bed and was soon fast
asleep. Then he was awakened again by a voice
calling: 'Samuel.'

Again he ran to Eli, saying: 'Here am I, for you
did call me.'

But Eli replied: 'I called not, my son! go and lie
down again.'

Samuel did as he was told, but once more he was
awakened by a voice calling his name. This time
when he went to Eli, the priest knew that the voice
Samuel had heard was God's voice speaking to him.

'Go and lie down,' Eli said, 'and if you hear the
voice again, say: "Speak, Lord, for Thy servant
heareth."'

Samuel went and lay in his little room again, and
when he heard the voice calling 'Samuel, Samuel,' he
replied as Eli had told him: 'Speak, Lord, for Thy
servant heareth.'

Then God gave Samuel a message to tell to Eli and his people.   In the morning when Eli asked Samuel what God had said to him, Samuel told him everything; Eli felt very glad that his little helper had been so quick to hear God's voice and would become a faithful servant of God.

A DAILY PRAYER

Father in heaven, help Thy little children,
To please Thee ever in their work and play;
Help them to be truthful, gentle, kind and loving,
To be like Jesus, and follow Him alway.

DAVID THE SHEPHERD

1 Samuel **16**. 23.

DAVID was a farmer's son in Bethlehem. He lived in a white, flat-roofed farm-house with his father Jesse, and his seven elder brothers.

When David was big enough, Jesse set him to mind the sheep and the little lambs. David was very strong and very brave, and he loved every sheep and every lamb in his father's flock.

He knew just where the greenest grass grew, and where the freshest water could be found. He never left his sheep without someone to care for them. He knew their names, and when they sought fresh pasture, he went in front to lead them.

He would call their names so lovingly if they lingered. If a little lamb was tired, he would carry it on his shoulders, or in the big pocket in front of his shepherd's cloak.

At night he would lead all the sheep into the sheepfold, where they would be safe for the night. Then he would light a fire and watch lest a thief or a wild beast come and steal away one of the sheep.

David had a sling which he carried at his belt, and a bag in which he kept smooth, round stones. Sometimes a lion came to try to steal a lamb, and sometimes a bear.

Whenever a lion or a bear came near, David would take a stone from his bag, fix it in the sling, and shoot, whiz! Bang! The stone would hit the wild beast's forehead, and over the animal would go.

Then David would hurry up, and, taking his club, would soon kill the animal. And so the sheep and lambs were always safe in David's care.

Sometimes in the day-time, when the sheep were quietly feeding, David would play a tune and sing. He had a harp with which he made sweet music.

David could hear a song in the sound of the brook, the whispering leaves and long grasses. He picked up his harp which lay beside him and began to play— he copied the soft whispering music of the wind in the oak leaves, the merry sound of the running water, the song of the birds in the branches.

All the lovely thoughts in David's mind came into the music. This is what he sang—a song of God, the shepherd of His sheep:

'*The Lord is my Shepherd: I shall not want.*
He maketh me to lie down in green pastures:
He leadeth me beside the still waters. . . .
I will fear no evil, for Thou art with me;
Thy rod and Thy staff they comfort me.
Surely goodness and mercy shall follow me. . . .'

THE SHEPHERD CHOSEN TO BE KING

1 Samuel **16**. 1–13.

ONE day David the Shepherd-Minstrel was out
in the fields of Bethlehem, minding his sheep.
Presently he saw someone running towards
him.

When the runner came near enough, David heard
him say: 'Samuel, the prophet of God, has come to
Bethlehem, and wants to see you.' David found
another shepherd to look after his sheep, and hurried
off to the city gate. Just inside the gate David saw
his father Jesse, his seven brothers, and an old man,
with long white hair and beard. This, he knew, was
Samuel.

Around Samuel were the old men of Bethlehem, listening carefully to all he said.

When David arrived, looking tall and handsome and brave, Jesse said: 'This is my son.'

Samuel said solemnly: 'God has chosen you to be king over His people.' David's seven brothers did not look very pleased, for Samuel had looked at each of them in turn before David came. To each of the seven the old prophet had said: 'Neither hath the Lord chosen you.'

Each of the seven was tall and handsome and strong, but Samuel knew that 'Man looketh on the outward appearance, but the Lord looketh on the heart.'

God had read David's heart and knew his thoughts. He knew that David would make a good king when King Saul had given up ruling. He told Samuel to anoint David king.

So now Samuel took his horn, filled ready with sweet smelling oil, and poured the oil on David's red-gold hair, saying to all the people gathered within the city gate: 'This is the king whom the Lord has chosen.'

But for a time David went back to the fields, and there, a shepherd lad, he watched the sheep and lambs and cared for them. When he could he played his harp and sang. Again this was his song:

'The Lord is my Shepherd: I shall not want.
He maketh me to lie down in green pastures:
He leadeth me beside the still waters.
I will fear no evil, for Thou art with me.'

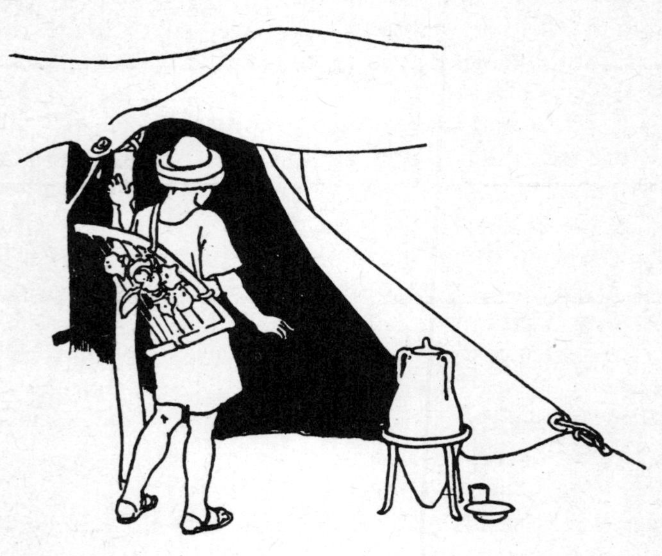

DAVID THE MINSTREL

1 Samuel **16**. 16–19, 23.

ONE evening, when David the shepherd arrived home, he found everybody excited, for strangers had come with a message from the king. David was called into the guest-room where his father was entertaining the messengers.

'This is David, my youngest son. He it is who plays sweet music on the harp.'

One of the strangers turned to David.

'The king is ill,' he said, 'we think it will do him good to hear sweet music—will you come to his camp and play on your harp to him?'

'My lord, I am the servant of the king. I will gladly come and play to him,' replied David.

Next morning David set off with the messengers to the king's camp. He led an ass loaded with good things from his father's farm as a gift to the king. His harp was slung on his back and around its strings he had wound lily flowers to keep the hot sun from breaking them.

After a long walk they came at last to King Saul's camp. One of the king's friends was waiting to welcome David.

'Come to the royal tent at once,' he said quickly. 'The king is very sad and ill.'

David took his harp and went into the dim tent. The king was lying on a bed of beautiful rugs. He had gold bracelets on his arms and wore a rich tunic, but his face was sad and pale.

David sat down on a low stool and drew his fingers over the harp strings. First he played the song of the wind in the oak trees, and the rustling of the tall grasses; then he played the tinkling song of the merry brook.

At first the king took no notice, but when David played the song that the birds sang in the oak trees he began to smile.

David then played all the songs he knew—the soft

tune he played to the sheep in the fold at night and
the merry songs he played at the harvest feasts in his
father's farm.

At last the king sat up, and spoke.

'Your music is lovely,' he said, smiling at David.
'It has sent all my sadness away. Will you stay with
me always, and play on your harp when I am sad or
ill, and make me well again?'

'I am the servant of the king,' replied David.
'Gladly will I stay and play to my lord the king.'

THE KING AND THE CRIPPLE BOY

2 Samuel **4**; **9.** 8–10.

DO you know anyone who is lame? How glad you are for your straight, strong legs and strong back! How eager you are to help any cripple you know!

David the Shepherd King once helped a cripple—this is the story.

There was once a little prince with a very big name—Mephibosheth. The little prince was the son of a dear friend of David's, Jonathan. Jonathan used to tell his little boy stories of his friend David—how he killed the lion and the bear—how he played his harp and sang to King Saul—how God had chosen him to be king, and Samuel had poured the anointing oil over his head.

Now one day Jonathan had to go away to the wars, for he was a general in the king's army.

Little Mephibosheth played with his nurse, and looked for his father's coming till one sad day. That day a runner came hurrying, breathless, with the news that Prince Jonathan was killed. The little boy's nurse picked him up in her arms and ran to take him to a safe place.

She thought that the men who had killed Jonathan might come for Mephibosheth, and hurt him. But running, the nurse stumbled and fell and dropped the little prince. He hurt his feet and became lame, and was never able to walk again without crutches. He found some friends to look after him, and stayed with them till he was a young man.

Then one day a messenger came to him and said: 'King David wants you to go to his palace.'

Mephibosheth felt shy and afraid, but he went. King David smiled kindly and said: 'Don't be afraid: for I will surely shew thee kindness for Jonathan thy father's sake. Thou shalt have all the land that belonged to him, and thou shalt sit at my table and have meals with me.'

Then David called a man to him and said: 'Prince Mephibosheth will make his home at my palace, and

sit at my table for his meals. Thou and thy sons
and thy servants must tend his fields, and gather the
fruits and the corn for thy master the prince.'

So the lame prince was happy once more.   He had
his own house and gardens and fields and servants,
and he sat at the king's table with David the Shepherd-
King.

THE KING
WHO BUILT THE TEMPLE

1 Kings **5**. 1–18; **6**. 1–9.

WHEN the young King Solomon came to the throne of Israel in the place of his father, David, he had one great wish—to build a beautiful house in which the people could worship God. He wanted it to be more beautiful than any house ever built, so that it would be fit for God Himself to dwell in.

So King Solomon talked with his wise men, and had plans made for the new house of God—or

Temple. He wanted it to be built of beautiful white stone, and the walls inside the house were to be made of sweet-scented cedar-wood. He sent a message throughout his kingdom for men to help in building the great new Temple. Soon there were crowds of stone-masons hewing stones and making them square and ready for the building.

Now there were no cedar trees growing in King Solomon's land, so he sent a message to King Hiram of Tyre, saying: 'Give me timber from the cedar trees that grow in your land, and in exchange I will send you wheat and oil to feed your people.'

King Hiram was glad to help in the building of God's house, and sent clever workmen with the timber to show King Solomon's men how to carve it into beautiful shapes and patterns.

All the work of hewing the stones and cutting the wood for the Temple was done some distance away, for King Solomon wanted God's Temple to be built without any noise or bustle or excitement. When the stones and beams were all ready, they were carried to the hill on which the Temple was to stand, and there they were placed in position almost in silence.

When the outside walls of stone were built, the inside of the Temple was lined with the sweet-scented cedar-wood, richly decorated with carved flowers, and palm-trees and figures of angels. The walls and floors were overlaid with gold, and the beautiful altar was covered with gold. Golden chairs formed a partition in front of the altar, and two golden angels stretched their wings across the sacred inner room of the Temple, in which was the sacred Ark.

The work of building this beautiful house for God took many years, but at last everything was finished. Then King Solomon called all the people to a great service in the new Temple. Standing before the altar, the king spread out his arms towards heaven, and prayed to God to be with His people when they worshipped in His House, and to bless them.

Then the people praised God, shouting and singing and rejoicing that they had been able to help in building the beautiful church to be God's dwelling-place.

After the service in the Temple the king held a great feast for the people to celebrate the opening of the building, and when all was over the people went away to their homes joyful and glad in their hearts for all that God had done for them.

THE BOY WHO
REPAIRED THE TEMPLE

2 Chronicles **24.** 1–14.

DO you remember the story of Samuel, the boy who was brought up in the Temple to be one of the helpers? Now we are going to hear a story about another little boy who lived in the Temple. His name was Joash, and he was a king's son.

Joash was only a tiny baby when he had been taken by his nurse to live with the priest of the Temple, Jehoiada. As soon as he was old enough the priest taught him to read and write, and talked to him every day about God's laws.

Often as they walked about the Temple buildings together Joash would say: 'Why is the Temple not looked after?   Why is this broken pillar not mended, and this door left lying on the ground?'

Then Jehoiada would say sadly: 'The people do not care about God's House now.   No one will help to mend the broken walls and pillars.'

One day Joash said: 'When I grow up I will build up God's House and make it clean and beautiful again.'

On the day that Joash was seven there was great excitement.   The priest called the people together in the Temple court, and before them all little prince Joash was crowned King of Judah.   The trumpeters blew on their silver trumpets, the musicians played on harps and cymbals, and the people sang praises and shouted: 'God save the King!'

The young King Joash went back to the palace to live, but he never forgot his promise to repair the Temple.

Before long he sent for Jehoiada the priest, and said: 'Make a wooden chest, with a hole cut in the top, and set it outside the gate of the Temple.   Then send a message to all the people to bring money to repair the Temple and make it clean and beautiful.'

Jehoiada did as the king commanded, and soon the people were flocking to the Temple with gifts of money.   They brought so much that the chest was quite full at the end of the day.   Each evening the king's officers carried the chest to his palace, emptied it, and took it back to the Temple. Soon there was plenty of money to start repairing God's House.

Then King Joash sent for stone-masons to build up the broken archways and pillars, and make the walls strong and firm. Carpenters came to make new doors and tables, and carve beautiful patterns on the wood-work inside the building. Metal workers mended the broken ironwork and brass vessels and candlesticks. Soon the House of God was strong and clean and beautiful again; and with the money that was left over, the king had beautiful gold and silver vessels and candlesticks made.

Then once more Jehoiada called the people together to the Temple courts. When they saw the strong walls and pillars, the great new doors of polished wood and brass, and the gleaming ornaments of gold and silver, the people shouted for joy. Then the king, the priests, and the people all sang together their praises to God.

ELIJAH AND THE POOR WOMAN

1 Kings 17. 1–24.

IN the long ago days there was a poor woman who lived at the seaside in a place called Zarephath. She had a little boy to love, but she had no husband to work either for him or for her.

The fields of Zarephath were bare and brown. There had been no rain for so long that the ground was baked hard. Neither corn nor fruits would grow.

The widow of Zarephath had no money and no bread. She had a handful of flour in the barrel, and a little olive-oil in the jar, and that was all.

Her little boy and she went out beyond the city

gate to look for sticks to make a fire to bake one little cake. While they were gathering sticks, they saw a stranger coming towards them. He wore a cloak of camel's hair, fastened with a girdle of leather.

He said to the woman: 'Please give me a drink of water.' And as she was going to fetch it, he called to her: 'Bring me, I beg, a morsel of bread in thine hand.'

The woman knew that the stranger was God's servant. Later she knew that his name was Elijah. Now she said to him: 'I have no loaf of bread, only a handful of flour in the barrel and a little olive-oil in the jar, just enough to make one little cake for my son and myself. After that there will be nothing left.'

Elijah said: 'Don't be afraid, but make me a little cake first. For thus saith the Lord, the God of Israel: "The barrel of flour shall not become empty, neither shall the cruse of oil fail, until the day that the Lord sendeth rain upon the earth."'

And the kind widow woman lit her fire. She mixed her dough, and baked a little cake of bread. She gave it to Elijah, and lo! In the barrel there was still a handful of flour, and in the jar there was still a little olive-oil.

She was able to mix a cake for her little boy and herself to eat, and even yet there was more.

She let Elijah, who was God's servant, stay at her house, and she gave him food. While he was there the barrel of flour never became empty, neither did the jar of olive-oil fail. There was always enough for her, her son, and for Elijah.

HOW GOD SENT THE RAIN

1 Kings **18**. 41–46.

WE live in a well-watered land, where the grass is always green, and where we always have water to drink. Do you remember the story of Elijah, and the widow and little boy at Zarephath?

There had been no rain for many months. The ground was baked hard by the hot sun, but neither corn nor fruits would grow. The children were hot and thirsty, but there was scarcely a drop of water to give them.

God's servant, Elijah, prayed to God to send rain. Then at last, one day he climbed a high hill by the sea to pray. He took his young man-servant with him, and they climbed to a place where they could see far out over the blue sea, and up over a great stretch of scorching blue sky.

Elijah knelt on the ground, bending his head down low, and prayed: 'Oh, God, send rain.' Presently he said to his servant, 'Go up now, look toward the sea.' The servant went up and looked and said, 'There is nothing.' And Elijah went on praying.

A second time Elijah told the servant to look toward the sea. A second time the servant came and said, 'There is nothing.' And Elijah went on praying.

A third time Elijah said to the servant, 'Go and look toward the sea.' So it happened three, four, five, six times. Always the servant replied: 'There is nothing.' And always Elijah went on praying.

But the *seventh time* the servant ran back to Elijah and cried joyously, 'Behold, there ariseth a little cloud out of the sea, like a man's hand.' Elijah knew now that the rain was coming. So he and his servant ran down the hillside.

The sky grew black with clouds and wind, and there was a great rain. It came down on the seeds of barley and wheat in the brown earth. The roots of the trees and every little plant drank it greedily. The mothers filled their water-pots, and gave cool drinks to their thirsty children.

Everybody said, 'Thank God for the rain!'

THE LITTLE MAID AND HER MASTER

2 Kings 5. 1–14.

THERE was once a little girl who lived in a country village in the land of Israel. One day soldiers came from another country, called Syria, burnt the farm-houses, stole the cattle, and carried away the best of the boys and girls to be slaves.

This little girl—we do not know her name so we will call her the little Hebrew maid—was taken away to a far-off city, Damascus. The general in charge of the soldiers, whose name was Naaman, saw her and said, 'She will make a splendid little waiting-maid for my wife.'

So the little Hebrew maid went to the palace where lived the great soldier, Naaman, and his wife.

She waited on Naaman's wife—went messages for her, brushed her long hair, fanned her with an ivory fan, brought water for her to bathe her hands. She thought her mistress the happiest woman in the world till one day she found her weeping.

Then she learnt that Naaman, the splendid soldier, was a leper. He would never be better and would have to go away and live by himself. The Little Maid was *so* sorry. Then she remembered someone in her own country whom God had made clever at healing sick people. His name was Elisha.

She said to her mistress: 'I wish my master would go to see Elisha, the Man of God. He would make him better.' The lady told her husband, and he told the king, and the king said: 'Go and see Elisha.'

So one day the Little Maid and her mistress watched Naaman ride away in his chariot, his servants with him, and bearing splendid presents of silver, and gold and fine clothes.

They counted the days till Naaman could return and the Little Maid told her lady over and over about Elisha, God's servant.

One day the sound of horses' hoofs was heard. The Little Maid and her mistress rushed to their window. 'It is Naaman, my master,' said the Little Maid. Presently Naaman came into the room. He was well!

'The God whom Elisha obeys has made me well,' he said. 'Elisha told me to dip in the River Jordan seven times. I did, and was healed. I offered Elisha presents, but he refused to take anything. He is a true servant of God.' No one there was gladder than the little Hebrew maid.

A PRAYER TO LEARN

Lord of little children, Father kind and dear,
Bless our little brothers, whether far or near.

HOW AN AFRICAN HELPED

Jeremiah 38. 7–13.

THIS is a story of a black helper who lived in Jerusalem. You perhaps would not have expected to find a black man in Jerusalem, but Ebed-melech was a coloured servant in the king's palace.

Sometimes one of God's servants, whose name was Jeremiah, would come to see the king. Jeremiah used to tell the king the words that God spoke to him. Often the king was angry at these words. And the princes were angry too.

The princes tried to stop Jeremiah from speaking

to the king or the people. They persuaded the king to let them put him in a place where they thought he would die. It was an empty cistern. This cistern was used for storing water, but now was empty except for horrid thick mud at the bottom.

Poor Jeremiah was let down into the cistern with ropes. He was weak and ill, and he sank down in the mud.

Ebed-melech heard what the cruel princes had done, and the kind, black man was very angry. He was so brave that he went to the king himself about it. He said:

'My lord the king, these men have done very wrong in all that they have done to God's servant Jeremiah. He will soon die of hunger where he is.' Then the king commanded Ebed-melech, saying, 'Take several men with thee, and lift up Jeremiah out of the cistern before he dies.'

So Ebed-melech chose several helpers and got some strong ropes and some rags, and let them down to Jeremiah in the cistern.

The kind black man said: 'Tie these soft rags under your arms so that the ropes will not hurt you. Then fasten the ropes under your arms and we will pull you up.'

Then Ebed-melech and his friends pulled, and pulled, ever so carefully and steadily, till Jeremiah stood once more on the ground in the fresh air. Both Jeremiah and Ebed-melech thanked God that he was free.

THE PROMISED KING

Isaiah 9; 35.

MARTHA always liked the Sabbath better than any other day of the week. It was like our Sunday, you see, and was the day on which she went with father and mother to the big Synagogue. The boys of the village went there every day, to school, while Martha and the other little girls stayed at home and helped mother.

Martha looked at all the other people on their way to the Synagogue. Everyone wore their best clothes, and looked rather solemn. She held her mother's hand tightly as they went into the big cool church and climbed the stair to the gallery. From there Martha could see the rulers, and the preacher—and, near the pulpit, was daddy sitting with a group of other men.

When the time came for the reading, Martha sat very quietly by her mother's side.

The ruler of the Synagogue took a roll of parchment out of its leather case, carefully unwound it, and began to read. Martha listened very carefully. These were some of the words she heard.

'Unto us a child is born, unto us a son is given: and the government shall be upon his shoulder: and his name shall be called Wonderful, Counsellor, The Mighty God, The everlasting Father, The Prince of Peace.'

The ruler stopped for a moment, unwound a little more of the roll, and then went on:

'The desert shall rejoice and blossom as the rose. It shall blossom abundantly, and rejoice even with joy and singing. Then the eyes of the blind shall be opened, and the ears of the deaf shall be unstopped. Then shall the lame man leap as an hart and the tongue of the dumb sing; for in the wilderness shall waters break out, and streams in the desert.'

Martha did not know what all of it meant, but the words sounded very lovely. She kept saying to herself all through the service: 'The desert shall rejoice and blossom as the rose.'

On the way home she said to mother: 'Who is the Child who shall be called Wonderful?'

'He is the King whom God has promised to send us,' replied mother. 'We have been waiting a long time, but we know He will come one day.'

'Will He come on a war-horse?' asked Martha, 'with soldiers and chariots like the Romans? Will He live in a great palace and have many servants?'

'We do not know,' said mother, 'but *when* He comes He will bring peace and happiness to our land. Then, as you heard the ruler read, "the eyes of the blind shall be opened, and the ears of the deaf shall be unstopped."'

'Yes,' said Martha, '*I* know, "and the desert shall rejoice and blossom as the rose." I *do* hope the King will come soon, don't you mother?'

Mother's eyes shone as she replied softly: 'Yes, little daughter, I hope He will.' Then she added: 'Perhaps if you ask God yourself He *will* send us the King soon.'

GOD'S WONDERFUL PROMISE TO MARY

St. Luke 1. 26–33, 38.

LONG, long ago, the people of the world were watching and waiting for a King. It had been said that one day a little Baby would be born who would grow up to be a very great King.

He would be loving, wise and good, and He would help the people of the world to be good, too. Everyone believed that the King would bring great happiness into the world, and so they longed for Him to come.

In the little town of Nazareth there lived a young woman called Mary. She lived in a little white house on the hillside, and every day she had her work to do. There was corn to be ground into flour, cooking and shopping to do, water to be fetched from the well, and the house to be kept clean. Mary was very happy, often singing as she worked.

Now Mary had heard of God's wonderful promise to send a Baby King. On the Sabbath Day, when she went to worship in the synagogue church, she listened to words read from the Bible. Sometimes the words of the promise would be read, and that made Mary think a great deal about the little Baby for whom everyone was looking and longing. She often wondered to whose house God would send Him when the time came.

One day something very wonderful happened. As Mary was sitting in her little home, suddenly the room was filled with a bright light, and when Mary raised her head, she saw standing before her an angel.

As she waited, the angel said: 'Hail, the Lord is with thee, blessed art thou amongst women.'

Mary was afraid, but the angel said: 'Fear not, Mary. Behold thou shalt have a Son. His name shall be Jesus, and He shall be the Son of God.'

When Mary heard those words, her heart was filled with a great wonder and joy to think that she was to be the mother of the Baby King.

As the days passed after that, Mary went about her work with a glad song in her heart. She and her husband Joseph talked together about the Baby who was to come to them, and planned how they would love and care for Him.

THE BABE IN THE MANGER

St. Luke **2.** 1–7.

MARY of Nazareth, about whom you heard in our last story was so happy! For she and Joseph had a lovely secret—God was going to send them a little Baby Son, whose name was to be Jesus. Each day Mary peeped into the wooden box where she kept the tiny garments she had made for her Baby; and in his workshop Joseph was very busy making a lovely cradle, strong and cosy.

One morning Joseph said to Mary: 'You must get ready to-day to take a long journey. To-morrow we must start to go to Bethlehem, which is many miles away.' So Mary packed up a bundle of rugs and some of the tiny baby clothes she had made (in case God should send her little Baby while she was away from home), and early next morning they left their little house to start the long journey.

Mary sat on the back of a donkey, while Joseph walked by its side, carefully guiding it over rough places in the road, so that Mary should ride safely. They had picnic meals by the roadside and at night they slept under the stars, or at a little country inn.

One evening, after several days' journey, they came within sight of Bethlehem. How glad Mary was, for she felt very tired. Soon they were in the crowded village street. Joseph knocked at several houses saying: 'Can we stay here for the night? We have come a long journey and are so tired.' But every time he got the same answer: 'I am so sorry, but we have no room here for any more people.'

Joseph was getting worried, for it was nearly dark, and Mary looked so tired. At last they came to a little inn. 'Surely we shall find room here,' thought Joseph, as he guided the donkey into the courtyard.

'Can we stay here for the night?' he said to the landlord. 'No, I am sorry,' replied the man, 'the house is full up. I haven't room for one more.' Then he saw how tired Mary was, and added in a kindly voice: 'But I have an empty stable where there is plenty of clean straw. You can rest there if you like.'

'Thank you,' said Joseph, 'we must take shelter there.'

The landlord fetched a lamp and took them to a stable in the courtyard. Mary unrolled the bundle of rugs and opened their little basket of food. When they had eaten their supper she lay back in the soft straw and Joseph covered her with a warm rug.

In the middle of the night Mary and Joseph's lovely secret came true. God sent them a tiny Baby Son: Mary wrapped Him in the soft baby clothes she had brought, and Joseph made a cosy bed of hay for Him in the animals' feeding trough.

Then Mary lay down again in the straw with her face turned towards her Baby Son, so that she could watch Him as He lay sleeping. Mary had never been so happy in her life!

THE BABE OF BETHLEHEM

St. Luke 2, 8–20.

THE very same evening that Mary and Joseph came to Bethlehem, three shepherds were preparing to spend the night on the hills outside the little town. They gathered the sheep into a fold enclosed by a rough stone wall, then sat down to eat their supper by the light of the wood fire.

Soon all was dark outside the circle of firelight made by the dancing flames. The shepherds drew their warm sheepskin cloaks close round them as they talked. Perhaps they spoke to each other of the wonderful King Whom the wise men of old had promised should one day rule over their land, and bring peace and happiness to all the people.

Suddenly they were startled by a bright light which seemed to be shining around them. They were seized with fear and hid their faces, but a voice said: 'Do not be afraid, for I bring you good tidings of great joy, which shall be to all people. To-day in Bethlehem is born a Saviour Who is Christ the Lord. You shall find the Babe, wrapped in swaddling clothes, lying in a manger.'

As the voice finished there was a burst of heavenly music, and of angel voices saying:

Glory to God in the Highest,
Peace on earth, goodwill toward men.

The shepherds listened, hardly daring to look until the bright light gradually faded, and the voices had passed away. Once more the shepherds were in darkness, save for the light of their little fire. For a few minutes they were so amazed they could not speak. After a while one said in a low voice: 'Let us go at once to Bethlehem, and find the Baby.'

'Yes, yes,' said the others eagerly, and grasping their long staffs they hurried away down the hillside to the town.

The streets were empty and silent. No light burned in the houses at this late hour, but the shepherds soon found their way to the little inn where they knew strangers would stay. There, sure enough, in a corner of the courtyard, they saw a glimmer of light. Silently they crept across the cobbled stones, and peeped in at the stable where a tiny lamp was burning in a niche of the wall. There they saw a wonderful sight. Baby Jesus, wrapped in soft white clothes, lay smiling in the manger-cradle while Mary and Joseph bent over Him, their faces shining with joy.

The shepherds crept softly into the stable and knelt down beside the manger. Then all together Mary and Joseph and the three shepherds said a joyful 'Thank you' prayer to God for sending them the gift of a dear little Baby.

When the shepherds rose from their knees and left the stable, dawn was breaking in the sky.

Away they hurried to the hillside, their hearts filled with gladness. One or two people were already stirring in the village, and the shepherds told them their joyful news.

'Rejoice with us,' they cried, 'for the King has come. Jesus Christ is born in Bethlehem. Rejoice! Rejoice!'

THE STAR OF THE KING

St. Matthew 2. 1–11.

WHEN you look at pictures of the Baby Jesus, do you ever wish you could have seen Him in the manger-cradle, on His bed of hay?

This story tells of some travellers who took a long, long journey to see the Baby Jesus. We do not know their names. The Bible calls them 'Wise Men from the East.' The land of the East was a long, long way from Bethlehem, where Jesus was born. It was so far away that it would take many days of riding on camels to reach Him.

The Wise Men loved to go out at night when the sky was full of stars, and watch them. They were so wise that they knew the names of many of the stars and where to look for them.

75

One night they went out together, and they saw a star that they had never seen before, and the new star was very beautiful. They looked at it a long time, but they did not know its name.

Several nights they went out, and looked at the star. Then they said to one another, 'Surely this star means that a King is born.' One of them said: 'Do you remember, a king was promised long ago in the land of Judah. Perhaps this star is a sign that He is born just now.'

'Yes,' said they all. 'Let us follow the star and look for Him.'

They hurried home and got ready for the long journey. They packed food and water and tents and sleeping rugs. They chose splendid presents to take to the Baby King. Then they set off over the sandy desert.

It was a long, long way, but at last they came to Jerusalem where they thought the King would be born.

'Where is He that is born King of the Jews?' they asked, 'for we have seen His star in the East, and are come to worship Him.'

The teachers in Jerusalem looked in the old books and there they read: 'The King will be born in Bethlehem.' They told the Wise Men, who set off for Bethlehem.

In an hour or so they reached the city and found the little house where Mother Mary watched over the Baby Jesus, and where Joseph looked after both of them. It was evening, and the star they had seen in the East seemed to rest over the little house.

They gave the Baby their gifts, and knelt down and worshipped Him.

THE BABY IN THE TEMPLE

St. Luke **2**. 21–38.

BABY JESUS was still *very* tiny when Joseph said to Mary one morning: 'Let us take our little Baby to the Temple Church at Jerusalem, to say "Thank you" to God for Him.'

Mary was very glad to go to the Temple and soon had packed up some food to eat on the journey— little flat cakes of bread, sweet figs and dates and a large bottle of water.   Then she wrapped little Jesus in a soft warm blanket, while Joseph saddled the little donkey.

When all was ready Joseph helped her on to the donkey's back, and away they started, Joseph walking by the side with a strong staff in his hand to help him on the journey.

The road to Jerusalem was long and stony, and Joseph had to guide the donkey over the rough places so that Mary should ride safely on its back. She held Jesus carefully in her arms and often smiled and talked to Him as they went along. At midday, when the sun was very hot, Joseph found a shady tree by the roadside where they could sit down and rest and eat their lunch.

Then on they went again, and soon, from the top of a hill, they were able to see the beautiful Temple shining white and gold in the sunshine. Down the hill trotted the donkey, and up another, and they were nearly there.

Mary was very glad when at last they climbed the steps that led to the great porch of the Temple Church and went inside, where it was very cool and quiet.

Among the people in the Temple that day was one old man named Simeon, who often went there, for God had told him that he should one day see the Baby Jesus who should bring happiness to all men.

When he saw Joseph and Mary coming into the Temple with the Baby in her arms, his face lit up with joy, for he knew that here was the little Jesus for whom he had been waiting so long. He asked Mary if he might hold her little Son, and taking Him gently in his arms, he thanked God for letting him see the Baby who should bring happiness to all the world.

Then, after blessing little Jesus, Simeon gave Him back to His Mother, who was very glad and happy to hear what Simeon had said about Baby Jesus.

While they were talking an old woman came towards them from another part of the Temple. Her name was Anna, and she, too, had been waiting a long time to see little Jesus. She smiled at Mary, and took the Baby in her arms, and together they all went to say 'Thank you' to God for sending Baby Jesus.

How glad Simeon and Anna were that they had seen Jesus. And as Mary and Joseph walked softly out of the Temple and down the steps, they felt happier still, for they knew that God had sent their own little Baby to make the world a better and more joyful place in which to live.

THE CHILD JESUS AT HOME

St. Luke **2.** 39; **7.** 32.

AFTER Mary and Joseph had been to the Temple Church they went back to their own village of Nazareth, where they lived in a little square white house. It was a little different from most of the houses in the village, because Joseph had a workshop next to the house, where he worked as a carpenter.

In his workshop Joseph was very busy all day, sawing long planks of wood, planing them smooth, and nailing them together to make all sorts of things

for the people of the village and the farms around
Nazareth. Sometimes he made a chest in which to
keep clothes, sometimes a wooden bin for storing
corn, or a plough for the farmer to use in his fields.

When Jesus was old enough to walk, He loved to
go into Joseph's workshop and play with the curly
shavings, or build with the little blocks of wood
which fell from Joseph's saw.

Jesus grew bigger and stronger every day, and
soon wanted to help Mother in the little house.
When they got up early in the morning, Mary opened
the door wide to let in the bright sunshine, while
Jesus helped Joseph to roll up their mat beds, and
put them away on the shelf. Then He helped Mary
to get their breakfast of flat bread-cakes and olives
and figs, or ran by her side when she went to the
well in the village street to fill her big water-jar.

When Mary ground the corn into flour between
two large flat stones Jesus brought her the corn in
His little basket. Then He fetched some water from
the big jar to mix the flour into dough, and gathered
some sticks and dry grass to make a fire for baking
the bread.

Once Mary lost one of the silver coins that tinkled
on a band round her forehead. She fetched a lamp
and swept the room, while Jesus peered into all the
dark corners.

'Here it is, Mother,' He cried, 'it has rolled behind
the water-jar.' How glad Mary was that the precious
coin had been found!

Sometimes little friends came to the door and said: 'Please can Jesus come to play in the market-place with us?' 'Yes,' said Mary, 'if you will take care of Him.' 'Oh, yes,' cried all the children, and away they ran, taking Jesus by the hand.

In the market-place they played lovely games, running races, or 'catch.' When they got too hot to run any more, Jesus said: 'Now let's play at weddings.'

'Yes, yes,' cried the children, 'let Naomi be the bride, and John shall be the bridegroom.' The bigger ones brought out their pipes and began to play a merry tune, while Jesus and the little ones crowded after the bride and bridegroom laughing, singing and clapping their hands. What fun they had! Sometimes they played at funerals instead, and made a great noise pretending to cry and mourn.

When the children were all tired, they took Jesus back to Mary, saying: 'Thank you for letting Jesus play with us. We have had such a lovely game.' And as they ran to their own homes they thought how much nicer their games were when Jesus played with them.

THE CHILD JESUS
IN THE COUNTRYSIDE

St. Matthew 6. 26–30; 8. 20.   St. John 10. 2–4.

NAZARETH, the village where Jesus lived with Mary and Joseph, lay in a hollow of the green hills.

Jesus knew some of the shepherds who took their sheep to the hills to feed on the grass that grew there. One day He ran home to Mary, feeling very excited, after meeting old Judah, one of His shepherd friends.

'Oh, Mother,' cried Jesus, 'Judah says I may go with him to the hills to-morrow to mind the sheep. Do let Me go.'

So next morning Jesus got up from His mat bed very early, dressed quickly, and set off to find Judah. The shepherd was busy getting the sheep out of the fold when Jesus ran up, quite breathless.

'Come along, Jesus,' said Judah, 'we must climb the hill before the sun gets too hot.'

What fun it was helping Judah to keep the sheep together, and to see that they did not lag behind. Judah walked in front with his crook in his hand, but he often looked round, and if any of the sheep were straying, he called them by their names.

There were beautiful flowers growing in the grass, blue and red and yellow daisies, and tall, white and golden lilies. Jesus wanted to pick some, but He knew they would die if He carried them in His hand all day.

When they reached the top of the hill Jesus and Judah were glad to rest in the shade of an oak tree, while the sheep wandered about nibbling the grass. Judah opened a little basket he carried and brought out some food, which he shared with Jesus. While they ate, Judah talked about the animals and birds which lived in the fields; how the birds built their nests, and where to find the little foxes' holes and the rabbits' burrows.

Judah got up and went to help a sheep which had got caught in a thorn bush, and Jesus helped him to set it free. Then He went to bring back a little lamb which had strayed away from the others; later on they took the sheep to drink at a stream lower down on the hillside, and then they started slowly back to the fold.

'I will pick some wild lilies and take them back for Mother,' said Jesus. 'Look at these, Judah, they are more beautiful than a king in his robes.'

'Yes,' said Judah; 'and God Who makes the flowers so beautiful and feeds the birds looks after us and feeds us, too.'

When they reached the fold, Judah and Jesus stood at the door counting the sheep as they went in one by one. When the last was safely inside Jesus said good-bye to the shepherd, and ran off to the village.

'These lilies are for you, Mother,' He said, as Mary met Him at the door.

'Thank you very much, Jesus,' said Mary. 'How lovely they are!'

Before Jesus lay down to sleep He knelt down and thanked His Heavenly Father for the lovely day He had had, and for the flowers and the hills and the stream.

THE CHILD JESUS AT
THE SYNAGOGUE SCHOOL

St. Luke 2. 40.

EVERY Sabbath day (like our Sunday) Jesus went with Joseph to the synagogue (which was like our church) to sing hymns and to praise God. When He was six years old Mary said to Him: 'Now you will be able to go to school at the synagogue, and learn how to read and write.'

So next morning Jesus went with some of His

friends, who already went to school, through the village and up the hill to the synagogue. The teacher was waiting for them in his long white robe, and the boys went in quietly and sat down cross-legged on the ground in front of him. Jesus was a little shy at first, but when the teacher brought out the big roll-book of the Scripture and began to take off the covering Jesus forgot that He was a new little boy at school, and was soon repeating the verses after the teacher. Then the boys said each verse over again all together. When they had learned several verses the teacher rolled up the book and put it carefully in its case.

'Now what are we going to do?' whispered Jesus to John who sat next to him. 'I expect we shall have a writing-lesson,' replied John. He was quite right, for the teacher began to make strange marks in some sand. First the boys had to copy out the letters of the alphabet and then they learned to write some words.

Some of the boys who could write well had a tablet of wet clay on which they marked their words with a sharp stick. Jesus thought these big boys must be *very* clever to be allowed to use clay tablets.

The teacher was very kind and helped Jesus to spell out some more words. Jesus felt very glad when the teacher said: 'You will soon be able to read and write.'

When the writing-lesson was over, the boys gathered around the teacher who began to tell them the story of Baby Moses and the beautiful princess. Jesus thought it was a lovely story, and when the teacher said it was time for them to go home, He was quite sorry that there was no more school that day.

As Jesus ran down the hill, through the village street, to the little white house where He lived, He said to John: 'I like going to school *very* much. I should like to be a teacher when I grow up.'

Jesus said 'Good-bye' to John at the door of His house, and ran in to find Mary who was busy patching His torn tunic.

'Oh, Mother,' He cried, 'it's lovely at school, and the teacher says I'll soon be able to read.'

'That is splendid,' said Mary, smiling at Him. 'Perhaps one day my big Son will be able to read out of the roll-book on Sundays at the synagogue church.'

Then, for the rest of the day, Jesus would play in the carpenter's shop, or feed the birds that gathered round the door when He took out the crumbs that Mary gave Him for the chickens and pigeons after their meal.

THE BOY JESUS AT JERUSALEM

St. Luke 2. 41–51.

THE day that Jesus was twelve years old was a very exciting and happy one—partly because it was His birthday, but more because He knew that He would now be able to go with Joseph and Mary when they went to Jerusalem to the great Feast of the Passover.

At last, the great day came for starting the journey to Jerusalem. It would take them three or four days to get there, so Jesus helped Mary to pack up warm rugs to sleep in at night, and food to eat on the way.

They joined a party of Nazareth friends going to Jerusalem, as it was much nicer to have company on such a long journey.

What a lot of new things and places Jesus saw, and what fun they had at night when they lit fires by the roadside, and had supper, and then lay down to rest under the bright stars. Jesus watched the stars twinkling till He fell fast asleep.

Each day they went on, until at last from the top of a hill they could see the city of Jerusalem, with the Temple shining in the sunlight. How beautiful it was!

When they reached the city they passed through the great gate and into the crowded streets, and Joseph took Mary and Jesus to the little house where they were to stay.

Early next morning they went to the Temple to sing songs of praise to God with many other people. Jesus thought the Temple was the loveliest place He had ever seen, and He wanted to go there every day. When there was no singing He liked to listen to the wise men who taught the people in the porch of the Temple. He loved to hear what the teachers said about His Father, God, and He asked many questions.

Jesus was very sorry when Joseph said they would be going home next day. In the morning He got up early and went to the Temple for the last time. Mary and Joseph got ready and set out from the city once more. They thought that Jesus was with some of His little friends farther along the road, but when evening came, and they could not find Him anywhere, Mary said: 'Jesus must have been left behind at Jerusalem. We must turn back to find Him.'

So Joseph and Mary went all the way back, feeling very worried. When they got to the city they looked for Him everywhere until at last Joseph said: 'Let us seek Him in the Temple.' Joseph had guessed rightly, for there was Jesus talking with the wise men, and asking questions. Mary ran up to Him and put her arms round His neck. She was so very glad to find Him. 'Why did You stay here?' she asked. 'Your Father and I have sought You sorrowing.'

'You should not have worried, Mother,' said Jesus, smiling at her. 'I have been learning such a lot about our Heavenly Father.'

Then they set out once more for Nazareth, feeling very glad that they had found each other again.

FISHERMEN FRIENDS OF JESUS

St. Mark 1. 16–20.

HAVE you ever seen a fisherman? What was he doing? Was he mending his nets? Or making crab-baskets? Or was he painting his boat? Perhaps you went for a row in his boat on the blue sea?

When Jesus grew to be a man He worked in the carpenter's shop at Nazareth to earn bread and clothing for Mother Mary and for His brothers and sisters. Then when these were big, He laid down His tools and set off on His travels.

He wanted to tell everybody about the loving Heavenly Father Who clothes the lilies and feeds the birds. He knew He would need helpers, so He looked about for some men who would make *good* helpers. First of all He chose four fishermen. This was how it happened.

One day He walked by the Sea of Galilee, and He saw two fishermen who were brothers. Peter and Andrew were throwing a net into the sea in hope of catching fish.

Jesus stood still and watched them. Then He said: 'Come ye after Me, and I will make you to become fishers of men.' And at once they left their nets and followed Him. They were glad to be His friends and helpers.

A little further on two other fishermen, James and John, were in a boat mending their nets. James and John were brothers, and sometimes they went out fishing with the other two brothers, Peter and Andrew.

Peter and Andrew went on with Jesus, and were ever so glad when He stopped in front of the boat where James and John sat mending their nets. They listened and heard Jesus say to James and John: 'Come ye after Me and I will make you to become fishers of men.'

James and John left the boat and their nets and went with Jesus and Peter and Andrew. Not long after, Jesus asked another fisherman, called Philip, to come and be His helper. Philip came, so there were five fishermen who went about with Jesus.

We call these helpers who lived with Jesus, His *disciples*. He chose twelve disciples altogether. He chose them that they might be with Him and learn from Him.

Sometimes Jesus used their boat when teaching the people, who came together on the shore to hear His stories. The fishermen pushed their boat out a little way from the shore and Jesus stood up in it and talked to the crowd.

Sometimes the disciples went and taught people about the dear Heavenly Father. Sometimes they cared for the sick, as Jesus taught them. Sometimes they were hungry, and had no house to sleep in. But they were very happy, because they were with Jesus.

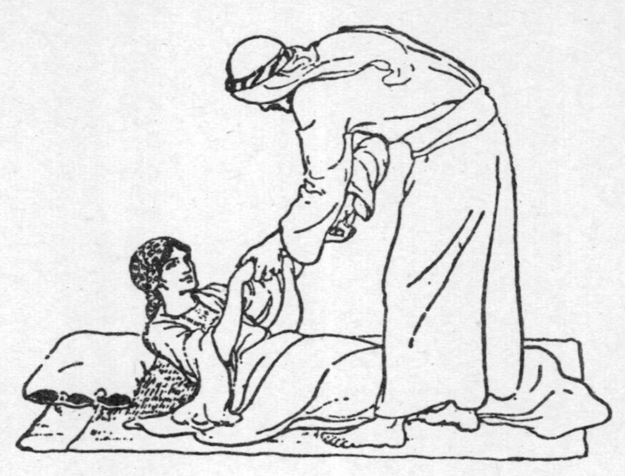

IN PETER'S HOUSE

St. Mark 1. 32–34.

JESUS often stayed at Peter's house at Capernaum-by-the-Sea. Peter's wife and Peter's boys and girls loved Jesus to come there. So did the old Grandma who lived there too.

One Sabbath Day when Jesus came home with Peter and Andrew from the synagogue, she was very ill with fever. Peter's wife came and told Jesus, and He went to her bedside, took her by the hand, and lifted her up. And at once the fever left her, and she got up and waited on them all.

I think she saw that Jesus had a very nice dinner that day, don't you?

That evening, just as the sun was beginning to

paint the sky red and gold, a great crowd of folks in Capernaum set off to find Jesus.

People who were well carried sick children in their arms, or led grown-up cripples and blind people to Peter's house. There were lame people on crutches, or carried on mattresses, there were little children in pain, but all of them were brought to Jesus.

He went out through the door and touched this sick laddie's blind eyes and made him able to see. He took that lame girlie's hand and told her to stand up straight, and her back became strong and well.

People threw away their crutches and leaped up in the air for joy that they were well again. The babies ceased their crying and laughed up into Jesus' face.

It was such a happy crowd that said 'Thank You' to Jesus just before the sun went quite out of sight. They went back to their homes and told all the friends how Jesus had helped them.

By and by everybody in Peter's house went to bed and to sleep. When it was still dark, Jesus slipped out quietly, and went out to the hills all by Himself. There He talked to the Heavenly Father, God, and God talked to Him.

Early in the morning Peter came to look for Him and said: 'All men seek for Thee.'

And Jesus said: 'Let us go into the next town that I may teach people there about God.' And so, with Peter and Andrew and James and John and Philip, and the other disciples, He went to many places, healing their sick and teaching the people.

JESUS IN THE CORNFIELDS

St. Mark **2.** 23–28.

HAVE you ever walked through a field of wheat at harvest-time? How tall and straight the golden stalks stand—you can scarcely see over the tops. If you stoop down you can look between the stalks and see the scarlet poppies growing here and there.

Perhaps you have picked one of the fat ears of wheat and rubbed it in between your hands until the hard yellow grains come out of the husks. Then, pff! you blow away the husks, and the grains are left in your hand. How good they taste when you pop them into your mouth and bite them!

It was the time of the wheat harvest in the land where Jesus lived. Jesus and His friends were going to the synagogue church to praise God for His harvest gifts, for it was the Sabbath (like our Sunday). They had a very long way to walk to the synagogue. They laughed and chattered as they went, and talked about the good harvest.

Just before they reached the little town of Capernaum they entered a large cornfield.

'Here is a fine field of wheat,' cried Peter, 'see how fat the ears are, and how tall the stalks.'

'Yes,' said James, 'the farmer will reap a good harvest. I should think he could spare us a few ears —I'm *so* hungry.'

James stopped and picked one of the ripe golden ears, and began to rub it between his hands. Some of the other friends did the same. When the grain was separated James held out his hand and the breeze blew away the light husks. Jesus laughed and said: 'It's a good thing that the law allows the hungry traveller passing through a field of wheat to pick and eat enough to satisfy his hunger, otherwise you would go hungry to the synagogue.'

THE FOUR FRIENDS WHO HELPED

St. Mark **2.** 1–12.

WHEREVER Jesus went, there was always a crowd of people to see Him and listen to Him.

One day in Capernaum the people heard that Jesus had come back to Peter's house. They hurried at once to the door to watch for Him coming out. Four friends met at the house and said to one another:

'If *only* we could fetch the man sick of the palsy to Jesus, He would make him better at once.'

'Let us go and fetch the sick man,' one of them said.

At once they hurried to the little house where the man sick of the palsy lived. 'We are come to take you to Jesus,' they told him as he lay on his bed on the floor. 'Jesus will make you better.'

'But I cannot walk,' said the helpless man. 'We will carry you on your bed,' said the four friends. 'There are four of us, and we will each take a corner of your bed.'

The bed was just a thin mattress, and they placed it on staves so that each friend could lift one corner, and the sick man lay quite safe.

Out of the dark, hot little house they went, the sick man blinking at the sunshine.

Presently they came near to Peter's house, but the crowd was so big they could not get through to Jesus. They stood still and said: 'What *shall* we do?'

'I know,' said one of the four. 'Let us climb up the outside stairs to the roof of Peter's house.'

The sick man lay very still on his mattress, and the four friends were very, very careful. They went slowly up the stairs, which were *outside* the house, not inside like ours. The roof, too, was flat like a table, so the man lay quite comfortably upon it.

Then one of the friends went for some strong ropes, and another set to work to make a hole in the roof. Soon they were back, and they began to dig through the roof. When the hole was big enough to let down the sick man on his bed, they tied a strong rope to each corner of the bed.

Then, very gently, they lowered the bed down, down, till it rested at the feet of Jesus Next the four friends heard Jesus speak so tenderly to the sick man. First He said: 'Son, thy sins are forgiven.' Then He said: 'Arise, take up thy bed, and go to thy house.'

The friends, watching, saw the sick man stand up, lift up his bed, roll it up, and carry it away. How glad they were!

THE RAISING OF JAIRUS' LITTLE DAUGHTER

St. Mark 5. 35–43.

LET us go back to Capernaum-by-the-Sea, where Peter and Andrew lived, and where Jesus often stayed.

At the synagogue church in Capernaum—the one to which Jesus went with Peter—there was a man called Jairus, who was a ruler or chief man in the synagogue.

Sometimes his little daughter went, too, with her mother. She was so glad when Jesus was at the synagogue. Twice He made sick people better when they were there to learn about God. The little girl liked to hear Jesus talk to the people in the synagogue.

Jairus loved his little daughter very dearly. She grew to be twelve years old, and one day he was very troubled, for she was ill. She did not run about and play or help her mother in the house.

She lay on her little bed with flushed cheeks and heavy eyes. She had fever, and she grew worse each day. At last her mother and father felt sure she would soon die unless something was done.

Jairus said: 'I will go and look for Jesus.' He went to Peter's house, but Jesus had gone across the lake. He hurried to the shore, hoping to see Jesus coming back.

To his joy Jesus stepped out of Peter's boat just as he got to the shore. Jairus knelt down on the beach, and said imploringly: 'My little daughter is nearly dead. *I pray Thee*, come and lay Thy hands on her, that she may get better.'

Jesus went with Jairus and a great crowd followed. When they were part way there they saw some friends coming who looked very sad. These said: 'Thy daughter is dead. Why trouble the Master any more?' But Jesus said: 'Don't be afraid,' and went on.

At the house there was a great noise—many people crying and wailing. Jesus went in and said: 'Why

make a noise and weep?   The child is not dead, but
sleeping.'

Then He went into her room with her mother and
father, and Peter, James and John, and taking her by
the hand, He said: 'Little girl, wake up,' and at once
she stood up and walked.

How thankful Jairus and his wife were to Jesus!

Then Jesus turned to the little girl's mother, and
said: 'Give her something to eat.'

FEEDING THE HUNGRY PEOPLE

St. John **6.** 1–13.

HAVE you seen the snowdrops begin to peep in your garden or the park? When they come they tell us that 'Spring is coming.' Soon the daffodils will wave in the March winds, and the fresh grass will spring.

Perhaps then we shall go for some long walks on sunny Saturdays. We may even have a picnic some bright, warm day. Do you like picnics?

In the land where Jesus lived, a boy once went a long, long walk on a bright Spring day. Other boys went, too. They went round the end of a lovely lake on which boats sailed. They hurried as they went, for Jesus was in one of the boats, and He was crossing to the other side. Would they be there to meet him? Yes, they got there just in time to see Jesus step out of the boat on to the beach.

The lad stayed as close to Jesus as he could. Crowds of people gathered, as they always did where Jesus was. The little lad listened to Jesus' kind words to them all, and watched while Jesus touched this lame boy and made him able to walk, and that blind woman and made her able to see.

The lad was so eager to see and hear that he even forgot he was hungry! His mother had packed up five little flat cakes of bread, and two little pickled fish for a picnic lunch. They were in the basket that hung from his girdle.

Evening drew near, and the people were tired and hungry. Jesus turned to Philip and said: 'Where shall we buy bread for these to eat?' Philip said: 'Two hundred pennyworth of bread would not be enough to give everyone a little.'

Then Andrew, Peter's brother said: 'There is a little lad here, and he has five barley loaves and two small fishes: but what are they among so many?'

Then Jesus turned to the little boy and said: 'Will you give me your lunch?' The lad gave it to Him gladly.

Jesus then told the disciples to make the people to sit down on the fresh green grass. Then He took the bread and the fish, and gave thanks to God for them.

Next He broke the bread and fish into pieces and handed them to the disciples, and the disciples handed them to the people. And there was enough for everybody, including the little boy. What a wonderful picnic that was!

THE DEAF AND DUMB MAN

St. Mark 7. 31–37.

THINK for a minute or two about your *ears* and what kind servants they are to you.

What wakes you in the morning? It is the sound of mother's voice calling: 'Time to get up, John. Wake up, Mary.'

Did you ever waken early and listen to the birds singing? Or perhaps your pussy comes and scratches at the bedroom door, or your puppy gives a bark to tell you he is awake.

The clock strikes eight, and you know it is breakfast-time. The postman rings the bell, and you run to take in the letters.

On the way to school, the motor-driver's horn tells you to be careful in crossing the road. Perhaps you have a school bell, and when it rings you know it is time to hurry. At school you hear your teacher's voice, the music of the piano for singing and drill.

I expect you would know your playmates' voices with your eyes shut. How merrily you can chatter and sing with them.

But suppose you could neither hear nor talk! You would be deaf and dumb. How sad that would be!

Once a deaf man was brought by his friends to Jesus. This deaf man was tongue-tied, too, so even if he could have heard he could not have spoken.

The deaf and dumb man felt afraid of the big crowd of people. Jesus knew he was afraid, and took him away by himself and smiled kindly at him. He put His fingers into the man's ears, and touched his tongue, to let the man know that He understood his troubles and wanted to help him.

The poor deaf and dumb man saw Jesus look up to heaven. The people around heard Jesus sigh, and then say a long word 'Eph-pha-tha,' which meant, 'Be opened.'

And straightway the man's ears were opened, and the string of his tongue was loosed. He could hear, and he began to speak plainly.·

And all the people were full of wonder, saying: 'He hath done all things well; He maketh even the deaf to hear and the dumb to speak.'

When the man went home he could hear his wife
and children when they spoke to him.   He could
answer their questions.   He could tell them: 'Jesus
gave me my hearing and made me able to speak.
How good He is!'

JESUS AND THE NOBLEMAN'S SON

St. John 4. 46–54.

IN another story we heard about the four fishermen of Capernaum who became the friends of Jesus.

There lived in the same town a little boy named Reuben, whose father was a rich nobleman.

One morning, when it was time to get up, Reuben felt very tired and hot, and had *such* a pain in his head. Poor little Reuben was very ill indeed.

Now the nobleman had heard how Jesus was going about the land helping to make people well and happy. He knew that when Jesus had been staying at Capernaum He had healed many poor people who were ill. As the nobleman saw his little son getting worse and worse he thought: 'I wonder if Jesus will come and heal Reuben. I must go and find Him.'

He crept softly out of Reuben's room into the bright sunshine in the courtyard. He called to a servant to bring him a horse and soon he was riding away to find Jesus. As he rode through the town he asked everyone: 'Do you know where Jesus is?' and at last someone said: 'Yes, Jesus is at Cana.'

Away rode the nobleman, for he knew that Cana was many miles away. It was nearly evening when he got there, but he soon found Jesus talking to some people in the market-place. The nobleman pushed his way through the crowd until he was near enough to speak to Jesus. He knelt on the ground and held out his hands to Him.

'Do please come and heal my little son,' he cried. 'He is very ill and at the point of death. Sir, come down before it is too late.'

Jesus looked at him kindly for a moment, then said gently: 'Go back to your house. Your little son lives.'

The nobleman's face lit up with joy, for he knew that Jesus had in some wonderful way healed little Reuben without even seeing him.

Thanking Jesus gladly he started for home at once, and rode all night. Early in the morning he saw some of his servants hurrying to meet him.

'Your son is living,' they cried excitedly.

'What time did he begin to get better?' asked the nobleman.

'About seven o'clock yesterday the fever left him,' replied the servant.

'Why, that was just at the time that I was talking to Jesus,' said Reuben's father, as he hurried on.

When he reached home Reuben was sitting up and looking quite well.   The nobleman told his little son how Jesus had made him well.   'How I wish *I* could thank Jesus,' said Reuben, 'I hope He will come soon, so that we can be His friends too.'

JESUS BLESSING THE CHILDREN

St. Mark **10**. 13–16.

WHEN Jesus left Nazareth to go on His journeys He made friends with the children in the villages through which He passed, and when they knew that He was coming that way again, they would run to welcome Him.

In one of these villages there lived a little girl and boy whose names were Ruth and John. They had a baby brother too, who was very small. His name was Peter. Ruth and John knew all about Jesus, for He had been to their village before, and they were always asking: 'Mother, when is Jesus coming again?'

'Some day,' mother would say. 'You must have patience.'

One day Ruth and John were very sad, for Baby Peter was ill. No one knew what was the matter with him, but he just cried and cried. Ruth sat on a mat in the cool shadow of the house, swaying him gently in her arms, and singing to him, but still he cried.

John went sadly down the street to look for one of his friends in the market-place. Soon he came running back as fast as his legs would carry him, shouting: 'Ruth, Ruth, who do you think is in the market-place?'

'Who is it?' asked Ruth.

'Why, Jesus has come,' cried John. 'You must come and see Him.'

'I can't,' replied the little girl sadly, 'cos I've got to nurse Peter, and mother is busy.'

Then mother had a wonderful idea.

'Suppose we all go, and take Baby Peter, too. Perhaps Jesus will make him well again. Don't you remember when He was here before how He healed the farmer's little boy, and made the blind beggar to see. I'm sure He will help us.'

So mother cuddled Peter up close, and they all hurried away to the market-place. Oh, what a crowd was there. All the men in the village had left their work and were standing listening to what Jesus was saying. There were some other mothers with their children too. Ruth and John could not see Jesus at all, so they tried to get in between some of the men; but mother could not follow because she was afraid her baby might get hurt. Some of Jesus' friends heard the scuffling and turned round angrily.

'You can't come here,' one of them said, 'Jesus is too busy to bother with children just now.'

Mother looked so sad, and Ruth began to cry; then they heard a kind voice saying: 'Let the children come to Me, do not stop them.'

The next minute Jesus was holding Ruth in His arms, and drying her tears. She soon began to smile, and when mother told Him why they had come, He put His hand on the baby's little head, and said: 'Don't worry, he will soon be well again.'

How happy they all were as they went home. The baby was sleeping quietly in mother's arms now, and the colour had come back into his pale cheeks.

'Jesus is our big Friend, isn't He, mother,' said Ruth.

'Yes,' replied mother, 'and you must be His friends too, and help Him when you are old enough.'

Jesus, Friend of little children,
Be a Friend to me;
Take my hand and ever keep me
Close to Thee.

Never leave me nor forsake me,
Ever be my Friend;
For I need Thee from life's dawning
To its end.

THE GIFT OF SIGHT

St. Mark **10**. 46–52.

POOR blind Bartimæus felt very lonely and sad as he sat by the roadside near the city gate of Jericho. All day long he had been there in the heat and dust, calling to passers-by to drop a coin into his wooden bowl.

He had sat there every day for so long that quite a large number of people knew him.

'Pity the blind!' he cried when he heard someone passing. 'Spare a coin for the poor blind man.'

But no one seemed to take much notice to-day. Presently Bartimæus knew why. He had heard everyone talking about Jesus. 'Jesus is in Jericho,' he heard one man say. 'He is doing many wonderful things. The people are taking their sick friends to Him to be healed.'

No one wanted to stop and talk to Bartimæus; they were all hurrying to see Jesus.

How Bartimæus wished he could go too. Perhaps if he could only speak to Jesus, He would give him his sight. But there was no one to help him to find Jesus.

Bartimæus sat there feeling very unhappy. Suddenly his sharp ears caught the sound of many feet, as though a great crowd of people were coming towards him. He listened carefully. Yes, he could hear voices, too—many voices all talking together. There must be a very great crowd. What could it mean?

'Why, of course,' thought Bartimæus suddenly. 'It *must* be Jesus. He is coming this way out of the city. Now is my chance. If only I can speak to Him. I know He will give me my sight.'

The people were quite close now. He heard someone near him. 'Who is it?' cried Bartimæus. 'Tell me who is coming.'

'Jesus of Nazareth,' shouted a man as he ran past.

There was such a great noise that poor Bartimæus wondered if he would ever make himself heard. 'Jesus,' he called loudly, 'Jesus, Thou Son of David, have mercy on me.'

'Be quiet, be quiet,' said someone roughly. 'Jesus doesn't want to be bothered with you.'

But Bartimæus shouted louder than ever: 'Thou Son of David, have mercy on me! Jesus, Jesus.'

All at once the noisy crowd became quiet. Then Bartimæus heard a clear kind voice saying: 'Bring him to me.' Someone touched his shoulder, saying: 'Be comforted, Bartimæus. Get up. Jesus is calling you.'

Bartimæus did not wait for any more, he sprang up, threw down his coat, and ran forward.

'What do you want Me to do to you?' asked Jesus.

'Lord, that I may receive my sight,' replied Bartimæus trembling with hope.

Jesus spoke again. 'Go your way,' He said quietly. 'Your own faith has made you see.'

As Jesus spoke everything became light to Bartimæus. He could see the blue sky, the sunshine, the crowd of people, and, best of all, the kind face of Jesus bending over him and smiling.

'Oh, thank you, thank you,' he cried. 'You have given me God's greatest gift, the gift of sight.'

IN THE HOUSE OF ZACCHÆUS

St. Luke **19**. 1–10.

IN the town of Jericho, in the days when Jesus was going about doing good, lived a rich man who had no friends. His name was Zacchæus, and he lived in a large house full of beautiful things.

He had plenty to eat and drink, and fine clothes to wear, but he was very unhappy. Everyone in Jericho hated him, for he was the chief of the men who gathered in the taxes for the king, and Zacchæus often took more money from the people than he should have done.

To-day Zacchæus felt specially unhappy, for he had heard how another tax-gatherer named Matthew had left his work to follow Jesus and be His friend.

'Oh,' sighed Zacchæus, 'how I wish I could have Jesus for *my* Friend too. I shouldn't be lonely any more.'

As he walked sadly towards the city gate he overheard two farmers from the country talking together.

'Have you heard that Jesus is coming into Jericho to-day?' said one.

'Yes, indeed,' replied the other. 'He stayed in our village last night, and I heard His disciples saying they would be in Jericho to-day.'

Zacchæus could have jumped for joy when he heard that. 'Jesus coming here to-day? Why, I must see Him, I *must*,' he said to himself.

Just at that moment Zacchæus saw a crowd of people coming through the city gate. They seemed very happy and excited. Whatever could be happening? In a moment Zacchæus understood. It must be Jesus! Now was his chance.

Zacchæus ran to meet the crowd, but the people pushed him aside angrily. He couldn't see anything at all, for he was much shorter than the other men, and they jostled him this way and that.

'I *will* see Jesus,' thought poor Zacchæus, and he started to run down the street in front of the crowd, to where a large sycamore tree grew at the side of a house.

Zacchæus scrambled up into the branches and waited breathlessly. Now he could see Jesus. Nearer and nearer He came—now He was standing under the tree—He was actually speaking to him, calling him by his name.

'Zacchæus, make haste and come down,' He said, 'for to-day I want to stay in your house.'

Zacchæus could hardly believe his ears. He almost fell out of the tree, he was in such a hurry to get down. He led Jesus away joyfully to his house.

'You are welcome, Master,' he said, as he led the way in.

He called his servants to bring food and wine for Jesus, and water to wash the dust from His hands and feet. But Zacchæus wanted to do more than this—he wanted to do something to show Jesus how much he wished to be His friend. Then suddenly he knew what he must do. If Jesus was going to be his friend he must be kind and honest and true, so that people would not hate him any more.

'Lord,' he said, 'I will give half of my goods to the poor, and if I have taken anything from any man wrongly, I will give him back four times as much.'

Jesus looked at him for a moment, then smiled and said: 'You have learned how to be My friend to-day, Zacchæus.'

THE WIDOW'S MITES

St. Luke **21**. 1–4.

ONE day Jesus went into the Temple, the beautiful Church in Jerusalem. He sat down near the place where the big offering-boxes were fixed, and noticed how the crowds of people brought money and dropped it into these boxes.

There were rich men with fat purses, who took out many coins and dropped them in one after the other. It was kind of them, but they still had plenty of coins

left in their purses, and in their money-bags at home.
They could pay for dinner and supper that day and
many days to come.

Presently Jesus noticed a poor woman who came
in all alone.   Her dress was plain and poor, and her
face was thin as though she was sometimes very
hungry.   Jesus knew that she was a widow.   Her
husband had died, and she had no one now to work
for her.

Jesus watched her.   She took out a poor, thin
little purse, and from it she took two tiny copper
coins called mites.   The two would scarcely be
worth one of our farthings.

Somehow Jesus knew that these two mites were
all the money the widow had in the world.   But she
put them in one of the offering-boxes with a smile,
and went away happy.   Most likely she would have
to go hungry until she could work and earn some
more money.   But she was glad to give to God.

Jesus called His disciples to Him and pointed out
the widow to them.   He told them what she had
given, and then He said: 'This poor widow gave more
than anyone else.   All the others who gave money
had plenty left.   She who had so little, gave all she
had.'

Ever since, people have loved to remember the
widow who gave her two mites to God, and the
loving words of the dear Lord Jesus about her gift.

THE CHILDREN WELCOME THEIR FRIEND

St. Luke **19**. 29–38.

WHEREVER Jesus was, there children loved to be. They knew without being told that He was their Friend.

On the day we remember as the first Palm Sunday, Jesus set off to go from Bethany to Jerusalem. It was not very far—just over the brow of the Mount of Olives and down on the other side, along the winding pathway.

Jesus had been staying at Bethany with His friends, Mary, Martha and Lazarus. They, and many others gathered to see Him off. One kind man lent Him his donkey to ride upon. Some of the men put their cloaks on the donkey for Jesus to sit upon, and on the ground for Him to ride upon. Some cut down feathery branches from palm trees and waved in the air, much as we wave flags when the King or the Queen passes by.

The boys and girls waved palm branches and called out 'Hurrah! Hosanna! Praise Him! Blessed is He that cometh! Hosanna in the Highest!'

They climbed to the top of the Mount of Olives and made a procession behind Jesus as He rode. Part way down the hill they saw the city of Jerusalem high on the opposite hill. Crowds of people, with many boys and girls among them, were coming to meet Jesus. These joined the procession in front of Jesus, and turned round to go with Him to Jerusalem. The boys and girls waved their palm branches and cried out 'Hurrah! Hosanna! Praise Him! Blessed is He that cometh! Hosanna in the Highest!'

Down the hill they went, and over the brook in the valley. Then up the hill they swept, through the city gates and into the Temple itself. There the blind and the lame came to Jesus and He healed them all. The children kept close to Him, watching all he did and listening to His wonderful words.

Every now and then they were so happy to be with Him, that they broke again into song. 'Blessed is the King that cometh in the name of the Lord: glory in the highest!' they sang.

When some of the grown-up men wanted Jesus to bid them 'Hush,' Jesus said: 'Have ye never read that the songs which our Father God most likes to hear, are the songs sung by little children?' And then the men could say no more.

THE MAN WHO LENT HIS ROOM·

St. Mark **14**. 12–17.

WHEN Jesus went to Jerusalem, He needed a room for the Last Supper and for a 'Good-bye' talk with His disciples.

There was a kind man in Jerusalem who lived in a big house with a large room on the flat roof. Outside the house were stairs that led to the Upper Room.

Jesus sometimes went with His helper-friends, the disciples, to stay, or rest here. And now the kind master of the house said he would lend Jesus his Upper Room for this Supper, and talk.

When Peter asked Jesus: 'Where shall we make ready the Supper?' Jesus said to him and to John: 'Go to the fountain in the city, and there shall meet you a man, bearing a pitcher of water: follow him.

And wherever he shall enter in, say to the good man of the house, "Where is the room where I may eat Supper with my disciples?" And he will show you a large upper room, furnished and ready.'

And the disciples went into the city to the fountain. There they saw a man carrying a pitcher of water.

Now water in Palestine is usually fetched by women or girls, so if a man carried a pitcher, they would notice him at once. They followed the man with the pitcher and came to the House of the Upper Room.

They asked as Jesus had bidden them: 'Where is the room where Jesus can eat Supper with His disciples?' And the good man of the house took Peter and John up the outside stairs into a large room. There he showed them couches and tables, with dishes and cups on the tables. At the door stood big water-pots filled with fresh water for the guests to wash their feet. There was also a big basin and a towel.

Peter and John made ready the Supper, and soon Jesus and the rest of the Twelve came to the Upper Room.

Here they had Supper together for the last time, and Jesus talked very lovingly to them all. He warned His disciples that He was soon going away from them, but that they must be brave and tell other people about Him.

He told them that He would make ready for them a place in the Heavenly Home, and that some day they should come and live with Him there.

THE FIRST EASTER

St. John 20.

THERE came a time when the friends of Jesus were very sad indeed, for the cruel rulers in Jerusalem had taken their dear Master and killed Him.

One of the friends of Jesus had buried His body in a rocky cave in his own garden, outside the city. Two days after, so early in the morning that it was still dark, Mary Magdalene, who had loved Jesus very dearly, came to the cave, bringing sweet spices and perfumes for the body of Jesus.

On the way to the garden she thought: 'How shall I roll away the heavy stone from the mouth of the cave?' Imagine her surprise when she reached the garden and found that the stone had already been moved! What could have happened? Someone must have been there and taken away her dear Lord! Poor Mary turned and ran back to find Peter and John.

'They have taken away the Lord out of the tomb, and I do not know where they have laid Him,' she cried.

Peter and John started to run to the tomb, and Mary followed, but John ran faster than the others and reached the tomb first.

He stooped down and looked through the low doorway into the empty tomb, but did not go in. Then Peter came up, breathless with running, and went right into the tomb. John followed. Yes, there lay the clothes that had been wrapped round Jesus, but nothing else! The two friends looked at each other wonderingly as they left the cave and went back home, leaving Mary standing outside, weeping.

As she stood there wondering what to do, Mary stooped down and looked into the cave. To her surprise she saw two young men in white garments sitting where the body of Jesus had lain. One of them said to her: 'Why do you weep?' Mary replied: 'Because someone has taken away my Lord, and I do not know where they have laid Him.'

Then a very wonderful thing happened. As she turned to go she saw Someone standing behind her. It was still not quite light and Mary thought to herself: 'He must be the gardener.' The Man spoke to her gently: 'Why do you weep? Whom do you seek?'

'At last,' thought Mary, 'here is Someone who can tell me where Jesus is.' Speaking eagerly, she said:

'Sir, if you have taken Him away, tell me where you have laid Him.'

But the Man said just one word—'Mary!'

At once she knew Who it was—Jesus Himself.

She could hardly believe her eyes; she was so happy that she could only say breathlessly: 'Master!'

How wonderful it was that Jesus was alive again and able to speak to her! All her sorrow was gone, for now she knew that Jesus would always be near. As she ran home to tell the other friends of Jesus what she had seen, her heart was singing for joy, and she kept repeating to herself: 'Jesus is alive. Jesus is alive for ever!'

THE FRIEND WHO CAME BACK

St. John 21. 1–13.

AN angel in the Garden where Jesus' body had been laid had said to Mary Magdalene: 'Go, tell His disciples that Jesus goes before them into Galilee. There shall they see Him.'

So Peter and John and the others went back to the Sea of Galilee, to the fisherman's cottage by the sea. Peter's wife was there, and the old Granny Jesus had healed of fever, and Peter's boys and girls. On the seashore their boats stood idle and their nets were dry.

Peter could not bear to be doing nothing, so one evening he said to the others, 'I go a-fishing.' They said: 'We also go with thee.' So seven of them climbed into a boat, pushed out into deep water, and let down their nets.   But though they toiled hard all through the night, they did not catch a single fish.

When the morning light began to show they turned their boat towards land.   They were tired and disappointed, and though they saw a Man standing on the shore, they did not look closely at Jesus.   Then they heard the Man say something: 'Lads, have you caught any fish?'   'No!' they called back.   Then He said to them: 'Cast the net on the right side of the ship and ye shall find.'

They let down the net as they were bidden.   Then they tried to pull it up, but it was so heavy they could not lift it.

John said to Peter: '*It is the Lord Jesus!*'   As soon as Peter heard this he jumped into the sea and waded to land.   The others came in the boat, dragging the net full of fishes.

When they were come to land, they saw a fire burning, with fish cooking on it, and bread ready. Jesus said: 'Bring the fishes you have caught.'   Peter then went and pulled the net upon the land, and there were a hundred and fifty-three fishes, and yet the net did not break.

Then Jesus said: 'Come and have breakfast.'   And He waited on them Himself, giving them bread and fish.

It was just like old times to be having breakfast with Jesus.   They were almost too happy to speak. They just looked and looked at Jesus, their Friend Who had come back to them.

PETER AND THE LAME MAN

Acts **3**. 1–10.

IT happened one morning when the Temple courts were filled with people going to the service. Peter and John were staying in Jerusalem, so they too left their work and went together at prayer time to the Temple.

The two friends walked through the courts and up the steps that led to the Temple door. As they were going in someone spoke to them.

'Pity a lame man,' said the voice. Peter and John stopped to look. Sitting on one of the steps was a beggar-man. He could not walk, nor had he ever walked; for ever since he was a baby, he had been quite lame.

Peter and John had often seen that lame man. They knew that his friends carried him every day to the doors of the Temple, but he had not come to pray. He could do no work, so he begged from all who entered the Temple doors.

Peter and John were sorry for the lame man. They wished they could make him happy. Suddenly Peter remembered Jesus, their Friend. *He* would have made the beggar-man strong and well. If only Jesus were with them! Then Peter thought again, 'But Jesus is here. He is with us all the time, although we cannot see Him.' The beggar-man was glad when Peter then spoke to him saying, 'Look at us.'

'He is going to give me money,' he thought.

But Peter said, 'Silver and gold have I none, but what I have I will give. In the name of Jesus, get up and walk!' Then he stooped down, caught hold of the lame man with his strong right hand, and lifted him on to his feet. The lame man had never stood upon his feet before, but when he felt Peter's strong hand and heard his kind voice he stood up. At once his feet and legs became strong, for all his lameness had gone. He could walk!

Peter and John stood watching while the lame man walked and jumped about for joy. Peter was full of happiness too. He was glad that he had been able to heal a poor lame beggar just as Jesus, his Friend, had healed people.

PHILIP AND THE STRANGER

Acts **8**. 26–39.

AMONG the followers of Jesus was a man named Philip, who loved his Master very much. Philip wished so much that *everyone* could hear about Jesus that he walked from town to town telling the story of how Jesus helped the poor and sick and blind.

One day he was in Jerusalem, wondering where he should go next. Suddenly he thought: 'I will go across the hills towards the town of Gaza and tell the story of Jesus in all the towns and villages as I pass through.'

Now it happened that a very great man was travelling to Jerusalem by the same road that Philip took. He was in the service of the Queen of Ethiopia, and had charge of all her treasure. He had travelled hundreds of miles from his home to go to Jerusalem, for he wanted to worship God in the great Temple.

It took *such* a long time to get there. As he rode along in his chariot he held a roll of parchment in his hand, and read aloud from it. The parchment book was part of our Old Testament, but he could not understand it very well—he did wish he knew someone who could explain it to him.

Suddenly he looked up and was surprised to see a man running towards him. It was Philip! When he reached the chariot Philip said: 'Do you understand what you are reading?'

'No,' replied the treasurer. 'How can I possibly understand it, unless someone explains it to me. If you know what the Book is about I pray you come into my chariot and tell me.'

So Philip stepped up into the chariot and sat down beside the treasurer. They held the roll of parchment between them, and Philip explained what the treasurer could not understand. Then Philip began to tell the African treasurer the story of Jesus —how He went about among the people healing the sick, making the blind to see, and the deaf to hear. He told how everyone loved Jesus for His gentle loving ways.

'Can't I be a follower of Jesus?' cried the treasurer. 'I would like to be His friend too.'

'If you believe in Him with all your heart, you are His friend,' replied Philip.

The treasurer was so glad that he had met Philip. He went on his way full of joy. What a wonderful story he would have to tell the Queen and her people when he returned to his own land!

DORCAS THE KIND HELPER

Acts 9. 36–42.

DORCAS lived in a beautiful town by the sea-side. Every morning when she opened the door of her little white house she could see the ships sailing by on the shiny blue waters.

Beyond the cluster of white houses lay gardens planted with orange-trees. How lovely the trees were in spring-time, when they were covered with sweet-scented white flowers. In autumn the golden oranges hung on them like lighted lanterns.

Dorcas was very happy when she walked among the orange-trees, but when she walked through the streets of the town she often felt sad. What a lot of poor little children there seemed to be running about the streets. Some of them had hardly any clothes at all, and looked so hungry. Some had just little ragged coats, others were crippled or lame.

One day, when Dorcas was returning from a walk through the orange gardens, a lovely thought came into her heart. 'I know Jesus would be sad to see His little ones cold and hungry. If I can do something to help *them*, I shall be helping *Him*.'

Dorcas hurried to the market-place, and bought some soft cloth and then went home to her house by the sea. She was soon busy making little coats and tunics, and in a few days she had quite a number. How happy she felt as she called the ragged children around her, and gave them each a little garment.

'Thank you, Dorcas,' they cried. 'Thank you.' And they ran home to tell their mothers.

Day after day Dorcas worked busily, and soon everyone in the little town heard how kind and good she was. But one day she did not feel well enough to sew. She lay all day on her mat bed, and when her friends came in to see her they looked sad, and said to each other: 'Dorcas is *very* ill. What can we do?'

'Let us send for Peter,' said one of the friends. 'Jesus has given him power to heal the sick. Perhaps he will come and make Dorcas well again.'

Dorcas grew worse, and by the time the friends had found Peter she lay quite still and pale. Some of the children and their mothers who came to ask how she was were told that she was dead.

At last Dorcas's friends came hurrying along bringing Peter. He climbed the steps to the upper room where Dorcas lay, and turning to the weeping friends, he asked them to go away for a while. Peter went into the room, and kneeling at the side of Dorcas, he prayed to God. Then he said gently to her: 'Dorcas, arise.' At once she opened her eyes, and when she saw Peter she sat up. Peter, taking her by the hand, lifted her up from her mat bed; then he called her friends to come in.

How happy they were to see Dorcas well and smiling again. The children shouted for joy when they saw her coming down the steps outside the house, and the mothers smiled and said: 'God has helped Peter to make Dorcas well again.'